THE MECHANISM

BY THE SAME AUTHOR

Poetry
Fairground Music
The Tree that Walked
Cannibals and Missionaries
Epistles to Several Persons
The Mountain in the Sea
Lies and Secrets
The Illusionists
Waiting for the Music
The Beautiful Inventions
Selected Poems 1954–82
Partingtime Hall (*with James Fenton*)
The Grey among the Green

Fiction
Flying to Nowhere
The Adventures of Speedfall
Tell It Me Again
The Burning Boys

Criticism
A Reader's Guide to W. H. Auden
The Sonnet

For Children
Herod Do Your Worst
Squeaking Crust
The Spider Monkey Uncle King
The Last Bid
The Extraordinary Wool Mill and other stories
Come Aboard and Sail Away

As Editor
The Dramatic Works of John Gay
The Chatto Book of Love Poetry

THE MECHANICAL BODY
and other poems

John Fuller

Chatto & Windus
LONDON

Published in 1991 by
Chatto & Windus Ltd
20 Vauxhall Bridge Road
London SW1V 2SA

A CIP catalogue record for this book is available
from the British Library

ISBN 0 7011 3760 6

Acknowledgements are due to the following, in which some
of these poems first appeared: *A Floribundum*, *The Orange
Dove of Fiji*, *Oxford Poetry*, *Poetry* (Chicago), *Poetry
Review*, The Poetry Book Society's *Supplement*, *Soho Square*,
The Stage, *The Times Literary Supplement*.

Photoset by
Cambridge Composing (UK) Ltd
Cambridge

Printed in Great Britain
by Mackays of Chatham PLC,
Chatham, Kent.

Contents

THE MECHANICAL BODY

THE MECHANICAL BODY

Lifting a curl of its hair mounted on gauze,
Inserting the key into one ear oiled with its own wax,

You were at first surprised by its yielding and weight,
The way you could wind it to a pitch of response.

The whole mass trembled with released springs,
A shuddering at the heart of it like laughter.

It stunned the player with its fringed opening eyes,
Making the onlookers instinctively draw back.

But it was all surface and expedient dollwork,
With hidey-holes for soul and coils for motive.

Unfinished the canyon of the stitched chest,
The mirror fragments, the panels of easy access,

The lacunae (. . .) (. . .) behind the knees,
The temporary leather, the hinged armpits,

Stencilled flowers on the linen ribs,
Your hands disappearing into glue.

Its sentiments worked on pulleys and punched rolls,
Tinny between bellows and horn-membrane.

The first hummings and trillings eased into
A pert sotto chirrup: 'Now then, Bertie!'

Little fans spun above the turning cylinders
And, with a tilt of the whirring chin and a slight click,

'Do it again, do it again, do it again' modulated
Into deeper more thrilling pronouncements,

And whatever you cared to say came flatteringly back
From a library of teeth shining and uplifted

As the vibrations in the throat sang out their triumph
Of elocution: 'Tonight – cherry tart!'

That face was all-important, the ivory jaw
Traced in one chisel-sweep from lobe to lobe,

The nose a guardian of resonance, vellum temples,
The powdered cheeks borrowed from mandarin hangings,

Best was the mouth, embroidered minutely,
Hidden the hooks and wires that trembled it into motion.

Their working went deep into the busy centre
Of emptiness, as from the flies of a theatre:

Oiled strands trundled from a central gear
Slung between the rolling pivots of the hips.

The sounding vibrato of the belly concealed
The whine of its continual working.

Its long strings leading to that simple ring
Through which they fanned, the ring contracted

And its webs and skeins diversified into
A pursed amusement or a moue of disgust

Or turned inside-out like a cat's-cradle,
Offering its watered-silk tapestry for kisses.

How the onlookers cheered! The thing was rooted,
Statuesque, a third larger than life.

It was gaunt with dust and tulle.
Bits of it glittered, even in the dark.

Great springs slowly lifted the padded knees,
Whiskery skirts leaking oil on to the floorboards.

And all the time was this ripple of felt and enamel,
This little jabbering of hammers and pulleys:

Its talking might talk you through till morning.
Your back was bruised from its attentions.

You thought of figureheads and oceans.
You thought of young mothers in their milk.

You thought of the egg-smooth backs of eyeballs
Staring unknowingly into the smoky caves of the future.

You thought of your life as a cheerful wager,
As a torn ticket of entry, a key to be used once.

You thought of cog turning cog turning cog,
The perpetual motion of the Last Chance.

You thought of the questioning of beauty in eternity,
Your hands at the controls, and celestial signs.

But as it wound down, its fingers barely twitching,
A tell-tale ticking from the ratchets of its joints,

There was nothing in the business but a blush,
A scattering of applause, a stillness.

And in that stillness, the postscript of a last
Creaking inch of clockwork was like a hollow laugh:

Hollow as the likeness of truth to a skull.
Hollow as the starlight pull of the doll.

SILHOUETTES

Sister, when I saw your toe whiten
Beneath the blade I thought it was already
Parted from pain and ready to be pitied.
I thought the business done, detached for ever,
Drained of the salt source we share, mere lump.
But that was only fear. The thing was still
Alive, though tensed and bent, like a small man
Almost used to being hurt, the arms
Clasped over the head, flinching from words.
And the scissors, for a moment, still had the skin
To cut. And, look! your hand still held the scissors.
Who said we had to be the shapes we are?
Or that those shapes are not desirable?

Sometimes in the lamplight I could think
Myself not more than shadow-deep from beauty.
Noses and chins on walls are graced a little
And get on terms. I could hug anyone
And never feel ashamed, or if refused
Refused with interest, fondness or respect.
Just a little does it. Like a cabbage:
Each leaf of such a thinness as you strip
To the heart, but that small centre is soon reached.
I think that everyone has once at least
Woken and wept themselves to sleep upon
A restless bed, alone and half an inch
From being hideous. Much more then, we.

When I heard your intake of breath, and the low
Growl of pain from your throat, I knew it was done,
Though cleverly you concealed that new object,
That part of you so like a grave of itself
With its grey little tombstone of a nail.
And you walked so proudly before the prince

As if in glory, with a baleful knowing enticement,
A smouldering glower as if bearing down on his mouth
With your determined mouth, and a small swagger
As without limping you placed each foot on the tightrope
Of the flagstones and no one to notice the slight
Leak at the gripping apron of the slipper.
O sister, though envious, how I prayed for you!

To fail is to want followers. But I
Was by your side, as sisters always are.
I took the scissors and put them in my sleeve.
(Were you to keep what you had seemed to win,
I knew that there was evidence to hide.)
It was not love, nor being a bride of blood.
It was not kingdoms, but a kind of justice.
For there was a fairy creature at the dance
Revolving by the beat, her skirts aflame.
The orchestra was hers, and hers the pulse
Of the night's bodily music, and the stars
Came out for her and for her tiny feet,
And I was wholly with you in revenge.

She took the perfect hours her shape allowed her,
But that was all. The truth has times that are
Unwilling servants of their wilful master
And if she changed her shape again, who knows
What spate of goblin nuzzlings might ensue?
Just once she could be goggled at for being
All she might ever want to be. The rest,
The future beyond the hours, the hours beyond
The future, are nothing but a demi-mask:
Blank as to insight, but cut out for speaking
As speaking is the staying of those hours.
Behind it is the dark we always face,
And silhouettes a dangerous game with scissors.

Now is my time. The crystal slipper wiped
And once again presented on its cushion.
The ceremony is a dream repeated,
Our whole life winding down, a second chance,
The last and only chance, the lifted mask.
What do I risk? I shall go down again
Into the hall with perfect staircase paces.
It might be nothing more than a raw place
At the heel, a scouring, a deliberate blister.
We lose such linings by the moon. A triumph!
For after all I am the elder. It is
Fitting. I am called. My foot is treading
For ever in its liquid sock of skin.

NEEDING FEAR

Have we always lived in the castle?
And how can it really be
That the dry moat is sufficient?
Two black ravens flapping
And the practice
Of bractice?

Danger has no future
And never had, whose spears
Rust in the rain outside.
Nor sneaking in of snakes,
Nor the defiance
Of giants.

And when the storm gives tongue,
Flickering from the mountain,
We may from walkways shout
Our answer, slam gates shut
With the clamour
Of a stammer.

No password hears its echo,
No secret touch through walls.
No one makes assignation
At postern for a parley
Nor bribes a sentry
For entry.

Whatever drenches towers,
Whatever grey skyscapes
Inch past the slit windows
It will be sunlight and singing
In the courtyard,
Like an orchard.

Walking there unthreatened,
Forgetting the man-thick walls,
It might be the playful ocean
That surrounds you sleeping with
The hot silence
Of islands.

But again, how can this be?
And must it always be so?
Surely one day we will wish
This sleight of stone we never
Quite intended
Could be ended?

Become uneasy with
Our quiet? Needing the fear
The walls were for? Needing
Their siege and (with whatever
Indignation)
Capitulation?

LESSON OF THE MASTER

His vision was titanic: the little we enact
Of comic calamity is at his whim,
Every misunderstanding, lack of tact,
Miraculous obtuseness, foretold by him.

Here are the maps of transatlantic drift
And dangerous friendship; the calculated stealth
Of evil, where culture is power and the gift
Of beauty a disaster, like ill-health.

He knew, as we do, how the physical
Acquires significance from our attention to it:
The wet boot held towards the fire, the full
Black hair. We come to see his meaning through it.

Fiction for him was, as for God, like playing
With the helpless questors of Eden. His face the face
Of Mrs Assingham, or Mrs Tristram saying:
'I should like to put you in a difficult place.'

If a charming vulgarian intended to strike
Some bargain with a snob, he would insist:
'You say you are civilised? Very well. I should like
To make you prove it.' He was an empiricist.

If pleasure beckoned, we could never follow.
If ghosts should appear behind the protective glass,
They too would prove our conversations hollow
And, like desire, would never come to pass.

Innocence is always shocking. It resembles
A clumsiness to which our heart goes out.
And we are stupefied. The hand trembles.
It is, we suppose, what love must be about.

Surely we realise that we have lost,
Way back, the path that might have led to joy?
Behind us is a threshold we have crossed;
Before us, other simpler lives we must destroy.

For after all, his humour comes down to this:
Betrayal is licensed by Bradshaw, and the sexed
Admirer foreshortens his future with a kiss
That leads, alas, to the closure of the text.

THE GRAVE AT RAROGNE

He wanted to be buried where he first
Admired the wind and light of the Valais
That like a perfect wine aroused a thirst
To satisfy that thirst, day after day.

Now from the south-west a different wind appears,
A disaffected spirit, randomly clad
In a fine red dust that shapes our seasonal fears
Of migraine, thunder, lost love, feeling bad.

Its visible robe is a hectic model of ours,
Shiftless, sly, or suddenly excited;
Stirring the fields that else would be making flowers,
Roses perhaps; turning up uninvited.

Were poems like red roses, made of earth
To be a moment's thought and then returned there?
Where did they shine, and speak of that strange birth
As though it were a purpose that they learned there?

'Will you not come? Oh, but the human soul
Craves joy and craves a deep eternity!
(That is philosophy). No other goal
Can tell us from the brutes, or sets us free.'

Will you not come? You are the night sky
Beyond the peaks, containing all the stars.
Things wait for you, these roses that may die
For the unpromised containment of your vase!

The graveyard, like a chattering balcony
The moment that the curtain rises, saw
The mountains as a wonderful wish to be
The thing that hushes us in sudden awe.

And every slab is silent now. Above,
The snows assemble. All the flowers hide.
It is the end of summer and of love.
The little church was honoured when he died

And handsome women came in furs and gave
The poet, as a token, one supposes,
Of all he'd given, dropping them in his grave,
(Although it was the depth of winter) roses.

DEAR BRUTUS

So you will start to count up to a hundred
And we will never know how far you got.
It is like the beginning of time. It is like time ended.
We don't know if it's real for you or not.

Had he already, then, begun to lose
You there among the shadows, knowing so well
The intimate and sexless role he chose
For both of you to play? We cannot tell.

We might think it disastrous, however pleasing:
You with no history, learning what to feel,
He with his dream, his easel and his teasing.
Perhaps it's not for either of you real.

Crack-in-my-eye-Tommy! It's real all right!
Just when you talk of putting up your hair
He has this strange distraction for a light
Like windows in a wood that isn't there.

How awful it would be to wake and find
You'd never been alive. That somehow Dad
Had simply imagined you. Yes! in his mind:
The thoughtful romping girl he never had.

But no, that can't be true. You feel it lift
Within your body like a branching tree.
It is the assembling blood. It is your gift.
It tells you you are Margaret, and free.

You didn't think it would embarrass him.
One, two, three, four . . . Hurry, Dad, come back!
As the spots fade behind the bosky scrim
There will be nothing for you both but black.

But who imagined whom? Who dreamed the child
And who the father? Was it a sort of pact?
Something within that wood is reconciled.
And now begins the terrible third act.

PHOTOGRAPH

The image of a possession, possessing and being
Possessed by a mystery, stares from this face,
One finger at the cheek, the eyes searching.
There is a double distance: hypothetical
Space, our space; and the studio's.

Light blinked into the brass and guarded chamber:
A faint perception of the curious way that
Something rehearsed could still be unexpected
Showed in the equal distance of her mouth
From either recognition or repose.

It might be almost words about to break
Out there, a smile's postponement of itself
In puzzlement, amusement half-dispelled,
Before the settling of the lips in trust
That ceremony is a silent thing.

And we have nothing but our privilege
To share this silence and its lineaments:
Low forehead, heavy brow and rueful chin,
Young as if for ever and the leasehold
Of its occasion's awkward fragile beauty.

She was not often much like this and now
Can never be again, but over and over
Looks through and at us from the knowledge that
This mystery has thought to touch her with,
A face outfacing all its history.

What has just passed is like the tree above
Her grave where birds shrilly debate their break-
ing from the clamour that they make, until
They burst from leaves and flock about the sky.
The moment afterwards is still to come.

THE SHIRES

Bedfordshire

A blue bird showing off its undercarriage
En route between our oldest universities
Was observed slightly off-course above Woburn
In the leafy heart of our sleepiest county:
Two cyclists in tandem looked up at the same moment,
Like a busy footnote to its asterisk.

Berkshire

Once on the causeway outside Steventon
I had a vision of living in willing exile,
Of living the knowingly imperfect life
But with a boundless and joyous energy
Like Borodin played by the North Berkshire
Youth Orchestra in its early days.

Buckinghamshire

A goose in the garden of the second-best pub
In Marsh Gibbon was busy doing its dirty toothpaste
And noisy, too, when a woman staggered out
Of the lounge bar into the deserted carpark
Saying: 'I could never think of the child at my breast
As anything other than a penis with a mouth.'

Cambridgeshire

The bird arrived. Nothing so stately-exciting
As Handel's dusky queen that was unspooling
Perhaps too loudly from a scribbling student cell,
But looped between the trees, a flash of green:
And only the having chanced to look just there
Could tell you it had ever been away.

Cheshire

There was a young woman of Cheadle, who wore her
  heart
Upon her sleeve, bright chevron! Oh, the keen-eyed
Men of Cheadle, as in the jealous month
When the registration numbers of new estate cars
Change all over wealthy suburban Cheshire,
And they picked out her heart with a needle.

Cornwall

The very last cat to speak Cornish had a glass eye
And kept a corner shop, selling shoe-laces and bullseyes,
Brasso and Reckitt's Blue. My great-aunt remembers
Buying postcards from him as a girl,
When George's profile sped them for a penny.
Aching to talk, he died of pure loneliness.

Cumberland

They play bezique in Threlkeld and they play
For keeps in Shap. And all the shapely clouds
Roll through the streets like weeping chemistry
Or cows escaped. And tea is served in the lounge
Over a jig-saw puzzle of the Princess Elizabeth
Beneath wet panes, wet mountains and wet sky.

Derbyshire

Once upon a time, in Derbyshire's leaking basement
Where you lie back in boats and quant by walking the
  ceiling,
A strange girl in the dripping darkness attached
Her damp lips to mine fast, like a snail's adherence
To cold stone in dusty nettles, and all unseen
The bluejohn slid by me: yellows, greys and purples.

Devon

You will never forget the fish market at Barnstaple:
Wet gills, doubled bellies, gleaming scales,
Shells like spilt treasure. And the cream there thicker
Than a virgin's dream, and Devon's greatest poet
Born Gay, on Joy Street, taught by Robert Luck:
It is the paradise of all fat poets.

Dorset

When the old woman entered the sea at Charmouth
And the great waves hung over her head like theatre
    curtains,
I thought of the sybil who charmed the rocks to yield
Their grainy secrets till history bore down
Upon her and the liquid world was fixed
Forever in the era of the fossils.

Durham

At the end of your battered philosophical quest,
The purity of Durham rises like an exhalation,
Like the stench of sulphur in a barrel. Birds
Build in the walls of the cloisters, disappearing into
    holes
Like black-robed devotees. Inside it is quiet,
The oatmeal crimping distant in grey air.

Essex

I had a vision in the dead of night
Of all the kitchens of commuters' Essex
Alight like the heads of snakes; and down them slid
The bored wives and daughters of the managers
Who were at the identical time arriving
On the ladders of their power and fatigue.

Gloucestershire

Armorial memorials reduced
To leper stone, forests to hedges, hedges
To sickled stumps where perch the songless birds
Of Gloucestershire, and vans require the roads
Before them in their headlights. No one speaks
In the time it takes to cross the greenest county.

Hampshire

Driving at evening down the A34
Like a ski-run, the sun a deiphany,
The car-radio a percussive Russian insistence:
Pure pleasure, pure escape! Past Winchester,
Unseen its stalking scholars, past everything,
Driving through Hampshire, driving for the boats!

Herefordshire

Alone between the Arrow and the Wye,
Wales to the west, keeping its rain and secrets,
I wandered in cider country, where the shade
Beneath the trees is golden red and noisy
With the jealous spite of wasps: Ariconium,
The poet Philips, his long hair combed out!

Hertfordshire

Hertfordshire is full of schoolmasters,
And archaeologists who are part-time poets.
Together they apportion past, present
And future among their imaginary admirers
In the form of examination papers, foul
Drafts, and labels of dubious information.

Huntingdonshire

Herds of deer are moving through the trees
Of Huntingdonshire noisily and rather
Slowly. An idle hand sweeping the lyre
Brings tears to the eyes of the moderately rich.
They will dip their hands in their pockets, gently dip
But not too deep. You've got to keep money moving.

Kent

Old men coming up to bowl remember
Other old men who in their turn remembered
Things that were hardly worth remembering
Through long still nights in Ashford, Faversham,
Sevenoaks and Tunbridge Wells and Westerham
Where even now the fields still smell of beer.

Lancashire

All the oven doors of Lancashire
Swing open on the hour, revealing vast
Puddings. After tea, the lovers stroll,
Their hands in each others' back trouser pockets,
Feeling the strange swell of the flexing buttock.
The sun sinks, and the Ribble runs to the sea.

Leicestershire

Cheeks of angels, lips compressed, donate
To brass invisible impulses of
Purely material breath: a county's children
Gather to create an overture,
While brothers and fathers leaping over hedges
Wind horns to their alternative conclusion.

Lincolnshire

M1, M18, M180: the roads
With their bight and bowline intersections sweep
North to Scunthorpe. Go further if you will
To where the Trent meets the Humber and Lincolnshire
   ends.
There, at Alkborough, you may draw breath
And if Nicky's at home she will give you a cup of
   something.

Middlesex

Middlesex is mostly roundabouts, the bright
Voice of five pm, insistent infotainment:
Fingers gallop irritably on the steering-wheel;
The nails make little clicks. Down the line
Of fuming stationary Volvos boys bully with headlines
That tell the drivers all about the place they have come
   from.

Norfolk

Norfolk is somehow inverted: it's all sky
With clouds as bulky as castrati or lines of Dryden
Sailing out above you, tinged with sunset.
Get as far as you can, but not too far,
Say to the Tuesday Market Place at King's Lynn
Where all the conveyancing is done in verse.

Northamptonshire

Once half-lost here, when only a map of sounds
Or smells could lead us from a wood, we came
At evening to horse-brass and low-timbered beams
Where the world had evolved to its great public state
And the men and women of Northampton, being
   counted
And with amber drinks, found themselves to be happy.

Northumberland

Traitors' county: from one end to the other
You can walk bright-eyed with never a second glance
From a stocky frowning people who move slowly
And mind their own business. For they have seen it all:
When the mist clears over Northumberland
It leaves squat towers, valleys scarred with lead.

Nottinghamshire

There is one red door in one slightly curved
Street in one nameless market town
That contains behind it for a moment an image
Of the planet's destiny: a girl stooping
To a hallway mirror, making her lips move
Into a theatrical kiss, a self-kiss.

Oxfordshire

The kingfisher has long flown. Along the Cherwell
The biscuit of bridge and college wall is blank
Of its image, but with a passing presence
Like a photograph taken with an open shutter.
This, we reflect, is just the sense of our life,
Aware of something the very moment that we miss it.

Rutland

Rutland is large enough for you and me
To stumble into as into a wood without being seen,
To tread its moss-starred carpet, enchanted
By the chipped china of the russulas,
Pink, grey, grey and green-grey, and red,
Peeping beneath the oaks, not far from Oakham.

Shropshire

Shropshire Blue, still made, the Lord be praised,
Tart veins that kept the Romans here and Housman
From the rope. The iron bridges lead you to it,
Farms knee-deep in cow. And if you stop off
In red-earthed Bridgnorth, that vigilant town,
Be sure your pint is not ungraced with cheese.

Somerset

A thousand airy harps! We hardly dare
To let out breath, for our imagination
Responds to these full-throated sounds as though
To the ranks of the ever-delighting dead, our wise
Visionaries, and this is the county of dreams
And of the moon's occult praesidium.

Staffordshire

Staffordshire is where you almost came from,
Darkened beneath burnt clay, perpetual dusk.
It is the housewife's dream, twinkling hearths
Bright with Zebo, scrubbed pumice steps
And, in the bathroom, a finger on the nozzle
And little lavender farts to begin the day.

Suffolk

I've had Leigh and buried St Edmunds,
Stowed Felix and Market and Upland,
I've been shut up in Boxton, found it painful in
    Akenham
And felt totally stupid in Assingham:
Carrying around one's valuable despair like a fleece,
To live in Suffolk is to suffocate.

Surrey

Flying in perfect formation above the sleeping
Cul-de-sacs of Surrey, you observe
The blocked pairing of houses, each with a garage,
Like epaulettes. What whisperings behind
The party walls! What eavesdropping, and what
Bad timing! Well done! Sorry, partner! Boom!

Sussex

Chalk pie, a quality of sun like laughter,
Distance predicted in hoof-beats: everywhere here
Is vigilance as well as cruel amusement,
That tempered island quality called sardonic.
From Rye to Selsey Bill, something is on offer,
A glittering spread, the bottom drawer pulled out.

Warwickshire

Driving to Wales I crossed a corner of Warwickshire
That seemed to be hardly space at all, the home
Of Dr Hall and his famous father-in-law
Or of magic woods where lovers were lost and found,
But simply the minutes that it took to tell
An unimportant story, now forgotten.

Westmorland

Once again the skies are open over the whole county:
From Clifton to Burton, from Grasmere to Brough,
The pubtalk steaming with anoraks and orange parkas.
But I can remember one solitary eye
Raging in silence in the dripping marsh,
Its dewy lashes spooning aphids from the air.

Wiltshire

In Wiltshire they are sending extra-terrestrial
Signals: what will the Venusians think of us?
Four-footed creatures who like to move in circles?
Let's hope they never noisily discover
That we are only half the men they thought us,
Stumbling at tangents from our glimpsed perfection.

Worcestershire

Oh darling, come to Broadway: there we'll take
Tea and scones and jam made from the plums
Of Pershore, perfect, pitless, palate-pleasing.
A stroll in the model street, a browse at Gavina's.
Then it's right foot down in the Volvo, plenty of Scotch
And the largest bed we can find at the Bull in
    Worcester.

Yorkshire

The brown teapot is always warming here
For there will be a time when you must come home
Though you be unknown except to the flowered dead.
On the moors the diagonal smoke rises
Like a bitter smile, tight but welcoming:
Cousin country, extra places for tea.

MASKS

One brumy night in early November when cheeks
Were cold to kiss and mist all loose in the grove
At the height of a coffee-table or a craven Jack Russell
So that you could not think of running there
Without dog-slobber or barked shins or simply having
Mysteriously missed your legs in the flooded field
We came back panting and laughing to a book-lined
  world

And you knelt on the rag-rug in your chimneyless room
Till the gas-fire played steadily like a small
Ceramic organ, the curtains not quite drawn.
It was at that moment when you reached for me, your
  hands
At my waist like an iris vase too heavy to hold,
Worth the admiring and nowhere to put it down,
That I stiffened and put one finger to your lips.

'Not now!' I was suddenly unreasonably distracted
By the thought of an expressionless face staring in
Like a guy, like the window's misty breathed mask
But without breath, the mouth and eyes mere slits,
Like a hooded face, both torturer and victim.
I said: 'If we pay him will he go away?'
But you said there was no one and you looked severe.

I couldn't keep up my appeal to this admonitory
Absence, or appease a self-induced scare
As though it were an eager High Street drunk
Stiff with dried spillings and a crooked smile
Leaning from the wall: 'Miss, a word with you!'
An old guy, who smelled of need and sorrow,
Sad adult, little father, burned father!

When you poured two tiny gins I was aghast
At the mockery of that painted mask's beseeching.
'Make it three!' But your lips smiled and tightened
In a weary ironical grimace and you tidied
The curtains' corners like a cloth on an invalid's tray.
You had seen real faces staring in – as so often
You stared, serene in thinking, stonily back.

Perhaps the face was your own reflection or
The result of a longing of mine too often repressed.
As the evening lengthened our eyes no longer met
At the explosions and my thoughts survived their
    puzzlement
As they lifted brightly up the chimney of the dark,
So many brave little wayward twinkling smuts
Skittering in smoke towards the hanging moon.

OFF THE RECORD

Three months to clear the creeper, twined about them
Thigh-thick in places, the amorous grasp of nature:

Pedestals in slime, and obelisks,
Great bevelled diadems and shafts, worn domes.

Most were tiered, sky-reaching, monumental.
Some lay tilted, overturned like idols.

Playthings of the gods, we called them, towers
Stubborned with iron, beasts and pinnacles.

Stone carved into frond-shapes that the skin feels
Inside it, stone blood or nostril, stone like sand.

Stone carved into space-shapes that the sun makes
On eyelids, stone shell or earlobe, stone like pearl.

So intricately carved that, when we hacked,
Nestlings escaped in fright like clouds of spice.

From one, tugging at tendrils we were surprised
By dripping from its lip a muttering of monkeys.

To civilise, that is our mission's purpose.
We have a name for everything we do.

Yet that deep vale now shorn of vegetation
Seemed more especially immensely sad,

A place designed for some forgotten purpose,
A place of energies, of interruption,

A place of understanding and of struggle,
A place of blank unusual namelessness.

Years in that dismal cirque, with knotted ropes
Charting relationships and distances.

We crushed new ink, and in the Record wrote
The names we gave, recording their positions:

Red: Empress, Cardinal, Rhinoceros,
Talia, Talia, Cardinal and Terror.

White: Elephant, Dabbaba, Concubine,
Talia, Champion, Talia and Terror.

Red: Mann, Mann, Mann, Giraffe and Mann.
White: Empress, Rhinoceros and Cardinal.

From the surrounding peaks (three miles of steep
Ascent) we saw much less, but saw more clearly,

Saw that position was relationship,
That space was time, and form a form of power.

This may be done to that, and that to this,
And something else, though not the first, to that.

The Record taught us so: volumes of love,
Of growth and illness, itemised in codes.

We have a name for everything we do.
We have a code which tells us how it's done.

But what of codes for that strange architecture?
Balm for its captures, charms for its every move?

Without impelling.touch it was itself
A code: we knew there were no codes for codes.

Rules for this god-game would describe itself,
Itself be understood outside all codes.

No reference to wrestling grips, the shrill
Cries of the breathless, or the stop of blood.

No round Os of surprise, the failure of
Attention, the missed opportunity.

No slackening of attack, the vertigo
Of daring irreversible decisions.

No sensations down the skin, collapse
Of knees, surrender of all tender surface.

From that pure height the pillars still outfaced
The morning mists and our interpretations.

After a week, forced to descend for water,
We closed the Record, all intent abandoned.

Of neighbouring tribes, flushed from the dwindled jungle,
There was nothing for the Record, little to say.

For some of us (too tired now to return
To fame, or bargaining with emeralds)

There was the prospect of a sluttish future
With their squat stolen daughters, who knew some tricks,

Peering between their legs as if to frighten
Wolves, their smiles turned into hideous groans

And sinewy honey-extracting tongues, so long
The tip could touch their anus like a wand.

Their language was a babble much like any,
With twenty different words for roasted oyster.

They said it used to be a paradise,
But we've no skill to make it so again.

Staring from wormy verandahs at the night,
We only note the creeper's slow advance,

Note pulsing in the neck, cries in the dark,
The sense of life as an unwilled postponement,

Note toothlessness, the monkeys come again,
And tendrils round the bases of those stones.

Unanswered questions: if they belonged to gods,
Then were they left behind through carelessness?

Or were the gods surprised? If so, by whom?
If a deliberate bequest, what then?

What could that war of white and red portend
And what its long unknown abandonment?

Gifts that we cannot handle may be stowed
Somewhere, but these we live beneath, like laws.

To civilise! Indeed. And then to dream
Of paradise, dream of the absent gods!

Perhaps these dreams are what we should preserve,
A way to write, and keep, the code of codes.

Otherwise I shall simply die like this,
Naming the millionth star then turning round

To creep from the verandah to the bed,
There to make love, and other useless games.

BIRDS

1

Two yellow finches pinned
Their hopes on cloud to share
In flight against the wind,

That massed undisciplined
Yet buoyant thoroughfare.
Two yellow finches pinned

All hope upon their twinned
Frail trust in wing and prayer
In flight against the wind.

The lifting current thinned
And let them fall, and where
Two yellow finches pinned

Against the swift thin-skinned
Invisible cold air
In flight against the wind

Thus sharply fell, it dinned
And raved the louder there;
Two yellow finches pinned
In flight against the wind!

2

At evening the swifts appear,
Flying round and round
In the air. In the late year

They are seen to scavenge here,
Swooping down to the ground
At evening. The swifts appear

To fall, but then they veer
Upwards and are found
In the air. In the late year

Light dwindles and they steer
Their course without a sound
At evening. The swifts appear

Black against the clear
Dusk. They flash and bound
In the air. In the late year

Only they have this queer
Ability to astound.
At evening the swifts appear
In the air, in the late year.

3
Birds of such a size,
No one can tell you what
They might be. Butterflies

Seem no smaller. Eyes
Pursue them to a blot,
Birds of such a size.

From field to wood they rise
Scattered and sharp as shot.
They might be butterflies

Whose wings are golden eyes,
But surely they are not
Birds! Of such a size

Birds were a surprise:
A lilliputian lot
They might be, butterflies

Grown brobdingnagian. Prize
Toys of nature, squat
Birds of such a size
They might be butterflies.

AWAKENINGS

I

Woken by the pale messenger whose soundless
   instructions they instantly convert
to the chatter of an exuberant code
   that defies half-sleeping enemies
with its power to cast a spell, these vocal
   units are reminded of their short
dangerous life. Elevated in leafy
   lofts from which earth's gravest law removes
the fragile and venturous alike, they
   look across the distances that part
them from similar havens and similar
   song, thinking: 'Light brings life nearer and
sound is a pattern of building. These towers
   are comfortable to welcome and
contain all that our chirrings and gatherings
   celebrate each morning.' So it goes
on, as we ourselves stir in that rare slumber
   which is the predicate of a long
and calculated pleasure, taken in no
   fear of shame or trespass, taken like
water from the lip of a tilted basin,
   taken in eagerness, without haste
or language. We, too, stir. And dream of falling.

2

Swart quartz dwarf! Unspeakable sound,
unthinkable idea whose
idiot eyes are digits like
Donald's which greed once lit into

a till! Poised at this minute to
inject its piled pulse into the
breathing dark and meters of sleep!
A daily call to dailiness

which is the minute's monument,
enemy of love's best prospects,
eraser of love's clouded thoughts,
regrets, intentions, memories!

It is than the round slow sun no
less of a monster, more of
a sprung trap down which swirl and gurgle
our modest and possible dreams

of ordinary waking and
touching, of turning one to the
other to defy its hectic
peremptory skittling jabber

that comes when it will come, like all
such minutes though unrecorded
that brought us once together in
our passion and divided time.

TWELFTH NIGHT

The last ten minutes of cake
   Stands in its crumbs.
Surviving almonds pose
   Like difficult sums.
Soon there'll be nothing left
   When a friend comes.

Birds on their clipped feet
   No longer play.
Golden fruit is plucked
   For the keeping tray.
The star that grazed the ceiling
   Is put away.

As, too, the tree itself,
   Naked, uncrowned,
Like an old phonograph
   Spinning round,
Weeping wax and needles
   Though without sound.

This image of our lives
   Seems pretty rough,
But what it might be saying is
   That all the stuff
That we've already had
   Is always enough.

ON THE MOUNTAIN

Grass scars
Of snow.
Drifts blow.
There's Mars!
Cloud bars
Still show
Though no
Bright stars.
Half-light.
A fox
Stilts by.
Then night
Unlocks
The sky!

BLACKBERRIES

Sister bramble, sprawled in the autumn hedges,
We think we can escape your wild embraces,
Your trailing skirts unpinned, the ragged edges
Bloodied with fruit like tiny damaged faces.
But always around the corner are those places
That something of stone or water makes you haunt.
We know your staring into empty spaces;
We recognise the shameless way you flaunt
Your secrets at each passer-by and taunt
With sulky mouthings and derisive clinging.
You are the summer's jilted bride, the gaunt
Neglected beauty who one day went singing
Out of the house, mindless of wind and rain,
To live from buckets in the filthy lane.

BOG

Kneeling for marshfruit like spilled
Beads bedded in displaying moss
I notice a licked frog dragging
His drenched fatigues up and through
The barring spears and stalks of orange
Bog asphodel as if in terror
Of unknown purposes, as though
I were a weight of sky, a whole
Universe of beak and gullet,
And not, as I am, a mere slider
And stumbler like him, damp to the hips,
Reaching for tussocks, scrabbling for almost
Nothing: these little speckled fruits,
Chill marbles of a forgotten tourney,
Aching playthings of a lost garden
That has always been mostly water,
A place of utter loneliness,
Terrain of the asphodel and of the frog.

PURPOSES

They totter heavily by
With orthopaedic necks
And pinched feet for purchase
Like night-wandering patients
Mad on a mountain cure.

Looking neither to left
Nor right they start and stop
And start, with little steps,
As if in 'twenties' skirts
On a drizzling promenade.

Dowager-bosomed, blinking,
Determined but unsteady,
Rapt but vacant, they admire
Only their own weight
And inscrutable purposes.

Everything else they ignore,
Night, day, boundaries,
Their white child bucking
And wriggle-tailed and ready
To escape, car-wash rain.

Everything is irrelevant
To their stately progress through
The atlas of nutrition,
Keeping the hill cropped close
To see where they are going

And pausing to raise the head,
Purse-lipped, in the blankness of bliss,
Chewing and pausing and chewing
Like a practised taster of Médoc
Almost sure of a vintage.

It may be that we too have
Such singleness of intent
Viewed from the right perspective,
Some alien lofty observer
Who would find us touching and comic.

Perhaps the knowledge would salve
Our own dim sense of confusion,
Sublime hauntings, pure puzzle.
Perhaps. How thankful we are
That we don't, and never shall, have it.

STONY ACRES

Something is gaping like a broken wall
In vacant fields. It must be the heart's spillage.
Yes, they've been down and up and down before,
These stones. This fresh collapse will take some clearing:
Migrant pieces needing to be flung back
In flinty protest; muddy chunks, and broken
Trapezoid wedges broadening to the shape
Of plates or blade-bones; wandering boulders; hopeful
Lintels whose weathered foreheads show how once
They coped; hurt shale; careless pebbles dancing
Dark down the hollowness inside; and some
Half-buried in the grass like plinths or armour
From fateful battles, immense in ancient moss.
Stemming this sprawl becomes a timely lesson:
A wall in place may be, like self-esteem,
A discipline of the damaged heart, yet somehow
With nothing much in sight that could escape
Or wander freely in, this dogged keeping
Of well-known lines and formal boundaries
Seems nothing better than an idle pleasure,
Balancing, wedging, stowing every crack
To cast long shadows on these stony acres.

HAUNTINGS

This is the greatest sadness, like Handel
Ascending a staircase to loud tribute
That is already worms although
We have to pretend that it is music.
And other sadnesses: that she
Whose whole existence is an answer
Has questions of her own that strike
Us dumb. Only our smile survives,
To haunt our quiet retreat from life,
And that abundant love bred out
Of loneliness which merely puzzles
Its busy, sensual, happy victims.

Inside a piano in a cottage
A mile out of the nearest village
A spirit in the jangling strings
Practises ascending thirds in
Moments of calculated stillness:
Not Peter Lorre's scampering hand,
Nor the ghost-print of Cage prepared
For his strange business, nor even Handel
Reduced to such vague finger-stirrings
As an ecto-presence might manifest,
Like picking the nose, but a ditsy shrew
To whom is allowed its privacy.

Do all such hauntings have precise
Explanations? Only the failure
That makes us feel pursued is never
Exorcised, for we ourselves
Become the terrible excuse
That it projects, our shadow-play,
Our mirror, our familiar.
Out there, though, every kind of music
Is ready to recreate the worldly

Heartache or triumph it once became,
And having once become it, will
Again do so, and yet again.

THE TWO TEAPOTS

The small teapot to the large teapot,
Stewed as a pond: 'When you last spoke,
Chuckling generously from your girth and glaze,
There were many who listened, who were friends.
Where are they now?'

The large teapot to the small teapot,
Clogged to a trickle: 'Peace, brother,
Your words are still warm and waited-for
By one who will be loved, though alone.
Be contented.'

THE WATERSPIDER AT EASTER

In these blue days between the palm and proof,
Learning almost that any theorem
Is possible if someone says it is
Whose very life is of that consequence,
I spend my time with time itself and you.

You speak of Thor endangering with his hammer
Inadequate heroes, having to be restrained
Like an enraged self-righteous householder
By milder gods. Further, in Isfahan
An eagle this week stole a picnicking child.

Let these be A and B, and now let C
Create the shape we recognise and fear,
A pattern of uncompromising law.
I do not find the matching shape about me
(Unless it is a mountain), only you.

And would that strange impelling finger touch
(Like taper to a paper) something so light?
A novelty like coloured fire? I guess
Divinity could never dare to be
(Nor shamed to) anything more than such as we,

An imitation of our ignorance
And little equilibrium. Surely
This is our best postponement, as we take
Our time and riot for our share of beauty?
The very idea gives us pause and hope.

And better theorems may disprove the worse
And what we reason be the milky head
And not the hammer, child and not the bird.
An image of the child, as yet unbroken!
An image of the breaking, not to be!

For even granite never thought of dying.
The pieces scarcely rock beneath the foot,
Cradles for water just before it freezes
And moss like ruined carpet after floods.
From cairns all sides descending are unequal.

Nowhere to go but down. We'll never find
By looking, so they say, but how to know
A way of seeing when the found is there,
A foolproof way to prove the obvious?
The famous answer is to kick a stone.

Here are those spurs and valleys where the green
Is parcelled out by legislating walls,
And stones move freely. The idea is constant,
Just as the weakest child or hero's foot
Still has some notion of the way to go.

Here argument is only exposition
Of truth like a summary narrative of nature,
The seething wells and the little locked churches
Like steps in logic taking us down the page
As the sun's sleep is aslant and westerly.

I want to trust in that as in the voice
Of the drowsing slabs and the wild echoes
Flying, flying, that catch the evening light.
Some suns will rise again, and we who will
Not last for long may not be discontented.

And by that holy pool, far from the mountain,
Where stooping is to touch, and touching is
A calculus of contiguities,
There straddles in its frail exampled stillness
Across a surface troubled but unbroken

The waterspider, miraculously skating
Upon the roof of liquid, sure as the hoof
Of a deer beats shyly over the nibbled grass,
Carw 'r dwfr, delicate stirrer of dreams,
Deer of the water, carw, deer of the streams.

Surely this is enough and will survive,
An image of the place that I have come to,
The irreducible, the secret source,
When time for three days takes its holiday
And all solutions are extemporised.

How kindly the creed of the actually virtuous
To stimulate no daunting disagreements!
For as you show, the good is to be sought
Beyond all rules that might empower its seeking
And that is all I need to demonstrate.

EATING THE STILL LIFE

The wind is in the stove tonight and we
Must not eat the still life. A shuddering
Passes across the chimney. The coals glow.

We made this civil practised silence out of
Thought that dwells on shapes. We know we must
Not eat the still life. Eyes look down and up.

The stove is booming like a basset-horn.
Apples in the basket glow. We know
We must not eat the still life. We draw.

We make these ceremonious shapes in silence
That lives in thought. We know we must not eat
The still life. Beauty is a translation.

Its burning rises into the night. Are these
Apples or faces that we draw? The fire
Leaps, and we must not eat the still life.

AT SUNSET

The fear of everything, the fear
Even to name fear, a kind of content
To sit in the spreading light, to sit
Helpless like an exhausted mother at last,
Amused and perplexed at our most precious gift,
Sitting and watching it go.

No, the feeling is like a child's,
In fact is a child, waiting for a word,
The word that comes at the end of a long day,
At the end of all its ragging and play.

What word is it? Who knows?
Something between rest and a kept promise
All the more valued for the keeping,
Known long since and only half-resisted.

As on this very evening, noticing
Such a weird light against the wall:
Forgotten whatever I looked up from,
Forgotten the fatigue, forgotten the fear,
Forgotten in this sense of possession and stillness,
The stream loud after a recent rain
And the sun leaking like fire beneath the door.

IN TIME

Spring thickens the tips
With black-blobbed buds.
Burnt marshmallows at the grate
Is winter's regret
For all its sticky lips
When the stove's heart stops.

The earth's ungatherable
Suggestions of growth
Promise again that they'll last,
That all is not lost,
Winding the year from one spool
To another, reel to reel.

Look again. How they've grown:
On far elder
And bordering hawthorn a mild
Flourishing like mould;
From the warming stone
The nettle's cautious fan;

And these black buds on the ash
Seem to explode
Like a conjuror's device
Or massed voice
When brass and cymbals crash
And the word is made flesh.

TREE FUNGUS

Standing to attention by the wall that once divided
Cottage-ground from field-bits and the beginning
Of steep descent to a rabble of civilian oaks,
It never questioned or guessed what it might have
    guarded
But grew in girth, eased stones aside, spread boughs.

A gate-place disappeared and corners collapsed.
The wall was nothing much, for what was on one side
Knew it could just as easily be on the other,
And what sheep started continued with digging for
    buttons
And roots growing through bottles in that littered
    ground.

Already the ash wore its medals of lichen with pride
And round its base in October the tell-tale signs
Of superannuating *Pholiota squarrosa* clustered,
Yellow pixie fringes sprouting at its coat,
Little insistent fingers probing its weakness.

Then winter, signing off the year with its flourishes
Of slate-slithering wind, delivered its stroke
And the great shape hit the deck in a dead
Faint, thought by many to be its last,
Hinged from its roots in gaping mountainous splinters.

But still it lived, sap flooding through the flap
To send up spindly shoots at what were really
Downward angles from the recumbent trunk,
While the still-sprouting crown, disguised in grass
Offered unusual food to inquisitive sheep.

It couldn't last for ever, this suspended state,
Reduced in leaf-lift and soil-suction, in all
Standing and buoyancy that makes a tree.
Branches that tangled with cables had to be sawn,
Its stumps leaked, its whole scope was diminished.

Well, it is our fate to live with symbols
For just so long as we ourselves persist,
Old soldiers of the paced life, admiring
Old soldierly qualities wherever we find them,
Hoping for nothing beyond the daily horizon.

So when, as ever in April, once more this year
Its buds blacken at the tips of its stretched fingers,
We are pleased to stand on its collapsed shoulders
And stroke its wild clumsy arms with a touch
That intends encouragement, a calming of terror.

It is then that we notice a new growth, the invader,
Daldinia concentrica appearing at the wrists
And pulse-spots in a lavish globular blistering,
Smooth exuded bulges running into each other,
Of a mineral hardness and coppery invalid brown.

Is this to be seen perhaps as a kindly harbouring
Of a vagrant fruit-body by one with weakened resistance?
Or is it pure power, an edging-out of the host?
It's a fungus not seen before, not edible, not lovable,
But whatever a tree does it is still a tree.

HOPE AND HEARTS

In the brown garden
Where playing lost its shadow
Among the lonely trees

These pale children of November
Rise from leaves
To forbid the frost and burning.

Frilfralog round the oaks
Tipsy and teetering
Putting up parasols

Skirted and stiff as dolls,
Never so still a dance,
So haunted a step

Till limp they lie down
Spilling their frills
In a lavish sprawl.

Everything goes back to earth
But first it must dance,
Dance to exhaustion.

They are our strangest thoughts,
Music of a mood
That will always create them

A solemn raggedy dance
At the year's end
But still as our own games

Games of outlandish endeavour
Games of promising
Games of hope and hearts

And like their rules
Allowing all they allow
And sometimes unbroken.

TEMPO

Tendrils are playing for
Their lives. The squares are crowded.
It seems there's no voyage left
To make. The evening star
Shines on an impasse here.

The creeper's thickening grip,
The pressure on the centre,
Is a slow paying-out
Of time, like a long rope
Never quite tied up

That inches through the grass
Or lifts from water, dripping,
The only sign that somewhere
A hull, though motionless,
Will in the end break loose.

The lessening light can find
No space for shapes to fill,
The blocked diagonal
Cannot be seen beyond,
The vital pieces pinned.

And always this slight moving,
Buoyant, invisible,
Draining the heart away
When what we need is loving
With no sense of misgiving.

Much is already lost:
Leaf repeats leaf repeats leaf,
Darkness assails the green
With indistinctness, fast,
And we await the worst.

But even as we despair
We feel the increased weight
That signifies the pull
We have long waited for
Hour after hour after hour.

And it is not too late
To take whatever we have
When taking is more like finding:
The freeing move long-sought,
The flowering overnight.

THE MALVERNS

Loaded like pilgrims who go upon their journey
Simply to be divested of those burdens
   Once the journey has ended,
Slogging our bodies with nature as if to prove
That they are still themselves as natural as once
   We used to think they were,
We find ourselves with a route to read that looks
Like a rough map of hopeful lives circling
   Back to begin again.

Down we plod from the wandering wooded ridge,
Scanning the fields as pages of a volume
   That never fails to please;
Tracing raw furrows, flints turned up again,
Those well-worn characters once lying beneath
   The chapter of a harvest;
Or stumbling by a hedge, a finger in the margin
Of a square of working barley which the wind
   Excitedly describes.

Here in one corner is a bribe of sweet-briar,
Its sprawling tangle of confessional blossom
   Appeasing some wild god,
The laughing enemy of agriculture
And all predictability whose arms
   Rake in the little badges,
The pale petals pinned at the centre, and gather
The illicit grasses in its thorny hoops,
   A sprouting lair of roses.

We take a path left by the tractor's wheel:
Squat incuse treads baked to a bare legend
  The stalks grew up around,
We cross the vale in a whole lake of barley,
The feathery beards brushing our bare arms like
  Insistent regrets or children,
Until we reach the further slope, the last
Before the hills, our eyes distracted by
  Its illustrations of flowers.

The sky is enlarged, and such as hides birds in it:
Birds flattered by the sun; birds emulating
  A single blown cloud;
Birds at their equal ease and distance, drawing
A notional horizon where is only
  An indiscriminate haze;
While nearer, though less visible, the lark's
Hectic credo and the response from a copse:
  'Brilliant! Brilliant! Brilliant!'

Our circuit at last ascends the green worn spine
Of the enormous book whose covers are two counties
  Laid down on England once
By yawning millennia hauled off to their sleep.
And now along the linked and nibbled knolls
  From peak to reaching peak
We pace in five winds like funambulists,
In agreement to take precedence by five paces,
  Windy, not yet quite winded.

When we have become pure vacancy,
Escaped like thin breath from dropped jaws
   Into completedness,
There may be many images to crowd us,
Ungathered treasures, ungathered irritants,
   Many things left over.
But when the spirit is finally finished
With its false hopes and its remembrances
   And is at last at peace

I can imagine its decision, in absolute freedom
(The random and theoretical gift of choosing
   Just one more scene or story,
One last opportunity of self-creation,
A momentary careless embodiment
   For no particular purpose),
To find itself aloft on this ancient turf,
A high place that only once was ours, our bodies
   Almost blown away.